Country Flower Drying

❖ ❖ ❖

Beverly Olson & Judy Lazzara

 Sterling Publishing Co., Inc.   New York

Edited by Laurel Ornitz

Color photos by Nancy Palubniak

Library of Congress Cataloging-in-Publication Data

Olson, Beverly.
Country flower drying / Beverly Olson & Judy Lazzara.
    p.   cm.
Includes index.
ISBN 0-8069-6747-1.   ISBN 0-8069-6746-3 (pbk.)
1. Dried flower arrangement. 2. Flowers—Drying. 3. Plants—
Drying. I. Lazzara, Judy. II. Title.
SB449.3.D7045   1988
745.92—dc19   87-26705
                  CIP

Published by Sterling Publishing Co., Inc.
387 Park Avenue South, New York, N.Y. 10016
Distributed in Canada by Sterling Publishing
% Canadian Manda Group, P.O. Box 920, Station U
Toronto, Ontario, Canada M8Z 5P9
Distributed in Great Britain and Europe by Cassell PLC
Artillery House, Artillery Row, London SW1P 1RT, England
Distributed in Australia by Capricorn Ltd.
P.O. Box 665, Lane Cove, NSW 2066
Manufactured in the United States of America

CONTENTS

Introduction   *4*

1   Before You Begin   *6*

2   Plants—Descriptions &
    Drying Techniques   *10*

Color section follows page 64.

3   Ways to Use Dried Flowers   *91*

Index   *127*

INTRODUCTION

You don't have to live in the country to have a country flower garden. By growing everlastings and then decorating your home with the natural beauty of dried flowers, you can recapture the country along with its traditions. Whether you are interested in flower drying as a hobby or a profitable business venture, by reading our plant descriptions and drying techniques, you will learn how to grow and preserve all kinds of lovely flowers. Then, by reading the instructions that follow, you'll learn how to use them in arrangements and wreaths and in an array of other home-decor items.

Our method of drying flowers is the same method they used in colonial America. It's the air-drying method, a natural process by which the air evaporates the moisture from the flower or foliage. We prefer air drying versus other drying processes, such as those involving the use of silica gel or sand. Compared to foliage dried by these other methods, air-dried foliage is more durable and will last much longer (years as opposed to months). This is why air-dried foliage is referred to as "everlasting."

Air drying is easy—all you basically have to do is grow it, cut it, and hang it.

If you already enjoy growing plants and flowers, then you will be pleased to know how you can preserve your gardening efforts. If you are a novice at flower gardening, our list of plants and drying techniques should eliminate any apprehension you may have about growing and drying flowers.

You probably already have most of the supplies needed for air-drying the plants described in this book. If not, the few supplies you will need are very inexpensive.

1
BEFORE YOU BEGIN

Select the plants for your country flower garden from any of the foliage described in Chapter 2. Follow the planting instructions provided by your nursery or those shown on the seed packet. Statice, both perennial and annual (annual for more color variety), Baby's Breath (*Gypsophila*), Strawflowers (*Helichrysum*), and Globe Amaranth (*Gomphrena*) are especially hardy and easy to dry.

The number of plants you should grow for drying depends on the amount of time, effort, and space you are willing to devote to your garden. However, those plants we just listed will give even the most avid flower dryer a good selection of materials.

What if you live in an apartment or a house where there is no available space for a garden? Do not despair—there are many other ways of obtaining beautiful materials for air drying. For example, there are community gardens or vacant lots in many large cities that can be rented for gardening. Or maybe you are fortunate enough to have a veranda that receives an ample amount of sun so that you can have a pot garden. It's best to use fairly large pots with good drainage, especially if you plant perennials that have long root systems. Imagine a Baby's Breath plant growing in a large pot, or Roses, Ageratum—the possibilities and plant varieties are endless.

If you don't have a veranda, but

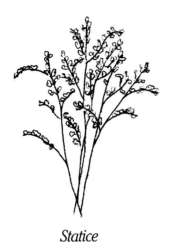

Statice

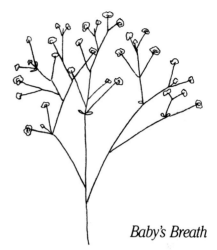

Baby's Breath

Strawflowers

Globe Amaranth

you do have windows that receive adequate sunlight, you can grow plants indoors in pots. Some commonly grown indoor plants are miniature Roses, Eucalyptus, and ferns. You might try growing an indoor herb garden, enriching your surroundings with their delightful aromas. A window box might be another solution. If you can't have one on the outside of the window, why not the inside?

If you live in a condominium or apartment complex, perhaps you could grow a rooftop garden. This is becoming a very popular practice in large metropolitan areas. Large pots are used, as well as wooden boxes constructed with good drainage. A rooftop garden can be a marvellous escape to the "country."

Do you ever receive or buy fresh flowers and then, when they wither, toss them out? Instead, you can dry their petals and leaves, and use them later for a potpourri. Ferns can be pressed. Don't let any plants go to waste.

Another option is checking vacant lots and areas where there is new construction. Chances are you'll find many types of wild flowers and grasses to use for drying.

Also, an abundance of plants grow wild in the country that can be harvested. It's always a good idea to carry a spare pruning shears in your car because you never know what plants you may come across while driving. However, when you are cutting foliage in the wild, you should be familiar with the laws since many plants are protected.

Of course, you can always buy dried flowers at local florists and crafts shops to use for dried floral decorating, but if you try some of the possibilities suggested here, it's bound to be much more fun, economical, and rewarding.

The proper environment for air-drying your materials is very important. It should be a dark, well-ventilated area—such as a garage, shed, attic, or spare room. A basement can also be a good location for drying flowers, provided it's not damp. In a place such as a garage, shed, or attic, you can pound nails into the rafters and then hang the dried materials from them. If you don't have an area where you can use nails or pegs, then a drying rack may be more feasible. This rack can be made in any fashion, as long as you can hang the materials from it upside down so that the stems and flower heads will dry straight.

If you have limited drying space, hang the foliage you have grown or gathered on coat hangers. Several banded bundles can be hung upside down on one hanger with Christmas-tree ornament hooks. A clothesline strung indoors can also be used for air drying. But remember, all foliage should be hung in a well-ventilated, dry area, away from sunlight.

As a general rule, you should hang your plants to dry for a minimum of 3 weeks before using or storing them. The few exceptions to this rule are explained in Chapter 2.

Glycerin can be used to make some foliage and flowers more durable. Thicker foliage and flowers, such as Eucalyptus and annual Statice, respond especially well to this procedure. Mix one part glycerin in two parts water. Initially, the water should be hot. Place the flowers stem down, in this mixture. Leave the flowers standing this way until the mixture is absorbed; this usually takes anywhere from 3 days to 3 weeks, depending on the type and density of the flowers or foliage. Check the plant for color uniformity before removing it from the solution. Then clean off any excess solution and hang the stems upside down to dry. You can buy glycerin at pharmacies or health-food shops.

There are also clear floral sprays that aid in preserving the color and life of dried flowers. These sprays can be found at crafts and florist shops.

When storing your dried materials, it's best to first wrap them in tissue paper and then gently place them in cardboard boxes. Keep your materials organized by labelling each box with the name of the foliage contained inside. Make certain that your materials are completely dry before you store them; otherwise, they will mildew. Always store your dried materials in a dry, dark place. If closet or cupboard space is at a premium, slide the boxes under a bed.

The few supplies you will need in order to get started in flower drying are a good pruning shears, a box of rubber bands, and 19- or 20-gauge florist wire. We suggest using rubber bands rather than twine to bundle the stems together because the stems will shrink during the drying process. The florist wire is used to replace the natural stems on plants with flimsy stems that will not hold up under handling.

Now let's get started!

2
PLANTS

Descriptions & Drying Techniques

Although many plant varieties are suitable for drying, this chapter describes those that we feel are most popular and readily available from garden shops and seed catalogues. For the sake of clarity, we have tried to list each plant by both its botanical and popular, or common, name.

New colors and varieties of plants are being introduced every year. Even though we have tried to be as thorough as possible, you will probably come across colors and names other than those we've listed here. Don't be afraid to experiment with other plants. You may well gain a lovely addition to your everlastings.

Some of the cutting and drying instructions in this chapter may seem repetitious. However, imagine how you would feel if you spent a lot of time and effort in your garden and then discovered you had cut your plants too soon or waited too long to cut them. If you have missed or ruined an opportunity because of improper cutting, the wait until next year's growing season will hardly soothe your spirits.

When you do begin to cut your plants for drying, always cut them after the morning dew has evaporated. Also, do not cut them right after a rain. You will find that the foliage will dry much better if you do your cutting on dry days.

Although there are recommended stages for cutting all of the flowers in this book, you should also cut a few of the flowers at other stages. A dried floral decoration consisting of some buds and partially open flowers interspersed among fully open flowers is always more interesting than one made up of flowers that are all at the same stage.

When you come to the plant descriptions, you will see a letter after each plant name. The letters mean the following:

(A) = annual   *(S) = shrub*
(P) = perennial *(V) = vine*
(B) = biennial   *(T) = tree*

An *annual* is a plant that completes its growth in one growing season. It will then die during the winter, and not grow again the following growing season. A *perennial* lives and blooms for more than one growing season. A *biennial* blooms the first spring after wintering one growing season. Then it usually dies the following season. Frequently biennials are planted in the fall to bloom the following spring.

Allium (P)

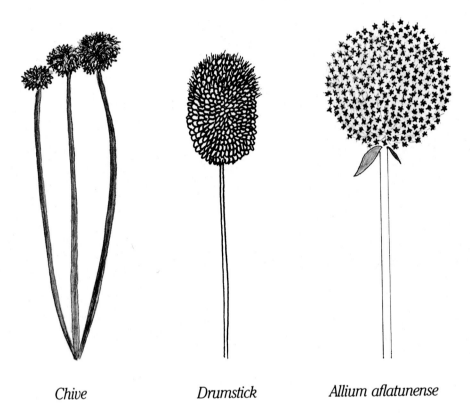

Chive   Drumstick   Allium aflatunense

There are numerous varieties of Allium, but here are a few of our favorites for air drying.

Chive (*A. schoenoprasum*) Commonly found in vegetable and flower gardens, this herb reaches a height of about a foot. It develops a lavender flower in late spring and blooms sporadically throughout the summer.

Drumstick Allium (*A. sphaerocephalum*) This variety grows approximately 2 feet tall, and has a purplish red 2-inch head tightly compacted on a sturdy stem.

Allium aflatunense This plant

has a large round head, formed by small star-shaped flowers. Its height ranges from 4 to 5 feet.

Allium giganteum Resembling Allium aflatunense, but larger, giganteum has a symmetrical head that can reach 8 inches in diameter.

For all varieties, cut the stems while the flowers are in full bloom; then bundle them together and hang them upside down to dry, or if the stems are sturdy, place them upright in an open container for drying. You may want to wear gloves when cutting some varieties because of their pungent odor and the moist residue they can leave on your hands.

Asparagus (P)

This description refers to both the everyday garden variety and Asparagus found in the wild. After you cut the Asparagus stalks for eating, the heads will bush out into feathery green foliage.

Cut this feathery foliage, bundle it together, and then hang it upside down to dry.

The foliage makes a good filler for arrangements, and can be used in place of some types of moss.

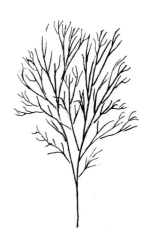

Asparagus

Baby's Breath
(*Gypsophila*) (A & P)

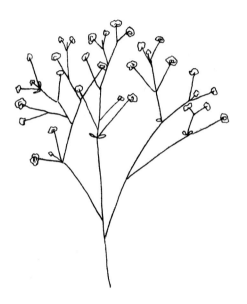

Baby's Breath

Gypsophila is an excellent filler for any type of floral arrangement. As it grows, the plant becomes a sea of small white blooms reaching approximately 3 feet in height. We grow the annual and perennial varieties in our flower gardens. Try experimenting with both to see which works best for you. A good perennial variety is Bristol Fairy. Pink varieties of *Gypsophila* are also available, but the white is a more versatile plant to use in arrangements.

You should cut the plant when most of the flowers are open, but before they turn brown. Bundles of *Gypsophila* can be hung to dry. Or, because of its thick branchlike stems, an entire plant section can be hung on a nail or hook for drying.

After you've dried the stems, you can dye them a color of your choice by soaking them in food coloring or a vegetable dye and then redrying. There are also colored sprays available at florist shops.

Bells of Ireland
(*Moluccella laevis*) (A)

This aromatic plant has green bell-like flowers with smaller white flowers inside. However, these small white flowers will drop out, leaving just the green bells. The plant grows to a height of 1 to 2 feet, and blooms in midsummer.

Cut the stems before all the white flowers fall out and the green bells begin to turn yellow. Then remove the leaves, band the stems together in small bundles, and hang them upside down to dry.

Note: Although this plant is an annual, we have had success with it reseeding itself.

Bells of Ireland

Bittersweet
(*Celastrus*) (V)

Bittersweet

Bittersweet is a vigorous climbing trailing vine with beautiful clusters of red-orange berries, and grows as long as 40 feet.

Cut the vines in the fall when the outer orange covers on the berries burst open, exposing the red berries inside. After cutting, bundle and hang to dry.

Note: If you bundle these vines together with ribbon and a bow, you can hang them immediately on a wall or door for decoration.

Boxwood, Korean Boxwood
(*Buxus*) (S)

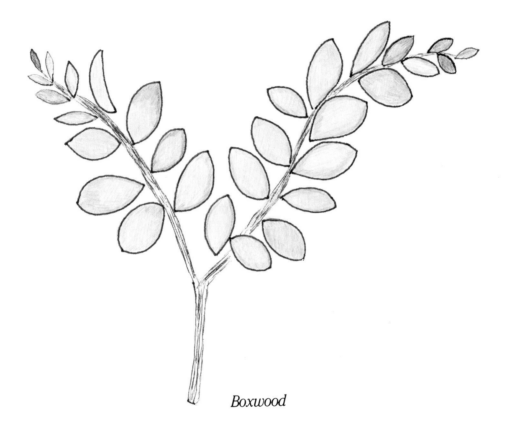

Boxwood

The Korean variety of Boxwood is the most hardy, and has small shiny dark-green leaves. Its branches can be cut and hung to dry or, while still pliable after cutting, wired to a wreath form and left to dry.

You can use these leafy branches as part of your Christmas-holiday decorating. Artificial red berries, available at florist and crafts shops, can be wired or glued to the branches.

Note: Unlike many shrubs, Boxwood is slow to replenish its pruned branches. You might want to keep this in mind when you're cutting.

Broom Bloom, Yellow Broom, Scotch Broom
(*Cytisus scoparius*) (S)

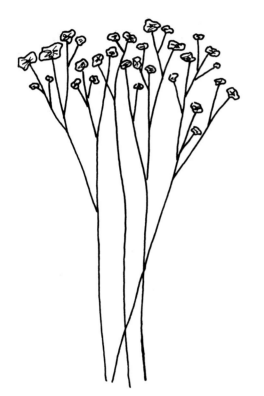

Broom Bloom

This shrub, which can't tolerate an extremely cold climate, has rich golden flower sprays, and reaches heights of more than 8 feet. These flower sprays dry naturally to a straw color. The blossoms and stems resemble those of Baby's Breath (*Gypsophila*), but the stems grow straight up, giving the plant a broomlike appearance.

Broom makes an excellent filler. Florists frequently use it when a particular curve or shape is required for an arrangement. A fresh spray can be wrapped with a wire and bowed to the desired curve. The wire is strung between the ends until the spray is dry. You can also hang this material upside down to dry.

Note: Although Broom comes in purple and pink varieties, usually the straw-colored Broom is dyed various colors for dried floral arranging.

Broomcorn
(*Sorghum vulgare technicum*) (A)

Broomcorn grows 4 to 7 feet tall, and resembles the corn we use for eating, except it has strawlike tassels instead of ears of corn.

Because of its popularity, Broomcorn seeds are becoming more readily available. The plant requires about a 3½-month growing period, so you may want to start seeds indoors, depending on the length of your growing season. After the danger of frost has passed, you can replant them outdoors.

In the fall, when the strawlike tassels turn golden and the seed heads appear, cut the tassels from their stalks and hang them upside down or lay them out flat to dry.

Note: Broomcorn can be a very interesting addition to arrangements and wreaths. It can also be bundled together the same way as wheat, secured by a ribbon and a bow, and then immediately hung on your wall or door for decoration. (You can even make your own brooms with Broomcorn!) Cut the tassels before the seed heads form. Then dry them for at least 3 weeks.

Broomcorn

Cattails, Reeds
(*Typha latifolia*) (P)

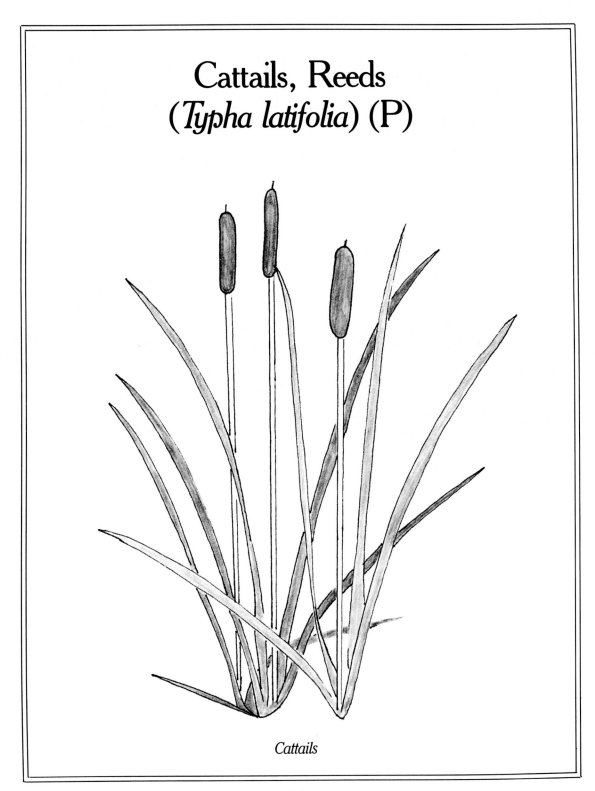

Cattails

Cattails are found along lakes and streams and in low wet areas. Depending upon the variety, this popular reedy plant can range from 1½ to 6 feet.

Cut the stem at a desired length during the late summer or early fall when the brown elongated tufts are fully developed. You should cut Cattails as early as possible. If you wait too late in the season, the heads will begin to deteriorate and eventually burst open. You can hang Cattails in bundles to dry, or stand them upright in an open container for immediate enjoyment.

Note: Cattails make a beautiful display either by themselves or combined with other dried materials. They work especially well if you want to create a masculine effect in an arrangement or a wreath.

Celosia (A)

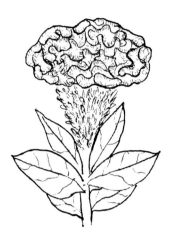

Crested Cockscomb

Crested Cockscomb (C. cristata) Many people prefer the crested Celosia over the plumed variety because it is more durable when dried. Heights can range from shorter than 6 inches to as tall as 4 feet, depending upon the variety. Colors include shades of pink, yellow, salmon, and red.

This plant can be cut somewhat late in the season when the crest, or ruffle, is fully developed. Two methods work well for drying. You can cut the entire stem, strip off the leaves, and hang it upside down to dry. Or, since the heads are large, you can divide them into desired sizes, place a wire through the ends, and then hang them upside down to dry.

When drying by either method, seeds will drop, so you may want to place a container beneath the plant to catch the seeds. When hanging the entire plant or stem upside down, you can band a paper bag around the flower head. This method will catch the seeds and protect the colors while drying. The seeds you are able to salvage from these drying methods can be planted the next growing season.

Plumed Cockscomb

Plumed Cockscomb (C. plumosa) The range of colors and sizes for this variety is the same as that for the crested Celosia.

There are two methods you can use for drying. You can cut the entire stem, strip off the leaves, and then hang it upside down to dry; or you can cut off individual plumes, bundle them together, and then hang them in the same fashion.

Note: The pink-to-red shades of Celosia retain their colors best when dried, whereas other shades have a tendency to fade.

Chinese Lantern
(*Physalis franchetii*) (P)

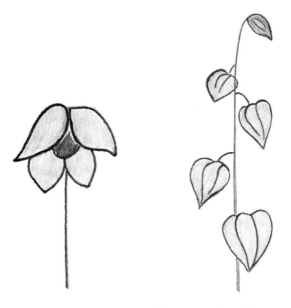

Chinese Lantern (flower and pods)

This plant has small white flowers that develop into balloon-shaped pods on stiff stems. The plant height reaches approximately 2 feet.

Cut the plant in the fall when most of the pods on a single stem are bright orange, strip off the foliage, and then either hang it in bundles or lay it out flat to dry.

You can also remove the pods from the stem and cut them open along their ridges, exposing their dark buttonlike centers. If you put a piece of florist wire into the base and center (do not go completely through the center), the pod will dry tightly on the wire and then open slightly into a petal-shaped flower.

Note: Chinese Lantern is a vigorous spreading plant with underground runners. You may want to keep this in mind when choosing its location in your flower garden.

Cornflower, Bachelor Button (*Centaurea*) (A & P)

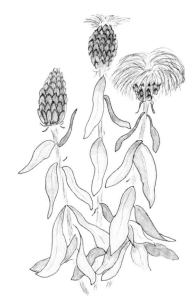

C. macrocephala

Centaurea is available in many colors and varieties. One of the showiest and most readily available is called C. macrocephala. This plant produces 4-inch yellow blooms, which are long-lasting and beautiful in freshly cut arrangements. However, it's the base of the flower that is used in dried floral arranging. The base is golden, and has a coarse texture. The plant reaches a height of 3½ feet. You can cut it before or after the yellow bloom appears. The base will be smaller if cut prior to blooming. After cutting the stems, bundle them together and hang them upside down to dry.

Note: For smaller varieties of *Centaurea*, cut the stems while the flowers are in full bloom, strip off the leaves, and then hang the stems upside down to dry.

Delphinium (P)

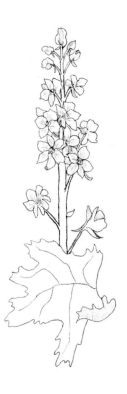

This plant has flowered spikes in shades of blue, purple, or white, and reaches heights from 2 feet up to 5 feet.

Cut during early summer when all of the flowers are open, except for the flowers that are 2 to 3 inches from the top of the spike. Band four to six stems together, and then hang them upside down to dry. You can also lay the flower spikes on a flat surface until they are dry. The flowers seem to maintain their shape better with this latter drying method. Delphinium may bloom again before the first frost, in time for another cutting.

Dock
(*Rumex*) (P)

Dock

Dock is a wild flower that is found almost everywhere. It grows in long spikes, which are varying colors during its growing season. You can cut these spikes during any one of these color periods. If you cut them in early summer, the spikes will still be green and the heads will be filled out. If you cut them in midsummer, they will be rosy beige to light brown. However, Dock is cut most frequently in the fall when the spikes are dark brown.

The shorter side spikes are normally used in arrangements. The whole spike is more appropriate for very large arrangements.

If you cut the spikes in the late fall when the stems tend to be stiff, place them in an open container for drying. If you cut them earlier when the stems are more pliable, hang the spikes upside down or lay them out flat to dry.

Edelweiss
(*Leontopodium alpinum*) (P)

Edelweiss

This plant has silvery foliage with white star-shaped flowers, and reaches a height of about a foot.

Cut the stems while the flower centers are still closed, strip off the majority of the leaves, bundle the stems together, and then hang them upside down to dry.

False Goat's-Beard, Meadowsweet (*Astilbe*) (P)

False Goat's-Beard

Astilbe has graceful flower spikes—in shades of red, pink, pink-salmon, rosy lilac, and white—which grow to heights of 2 to 3 feet. Most varieties will flower from June through September. This plant does best in a partially shaded, cool, moist environment.

Cut the spikes when the blooms are almost at their peak. Then bundle the stems together and hang them upside down to dry.

29

Ferns (P)

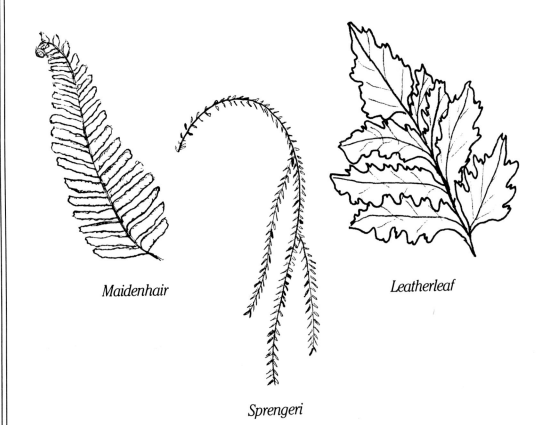

Maidenhair

Sprengeri

Leatherleaf

Good varieties of ferns to use for drying are Maidenhair, Sprengeri, and Leatherleaf.

Ferns are air-dried by pressing. An easy method is to cut the ferns at their base and then place them inside the pages of a telephone book. You can also place them between sheets of plain, smooth, uncoated paper, with a weight on top, such as a book. The ferns will be dry in about a week. You shouldn't place ferns between pieces of paper towel or tissue since they can stick to tissue and receive bumpy indentations from paper towel.

Feverfew
(*Matricaria, Chrysanthemum parthenium*) (A)

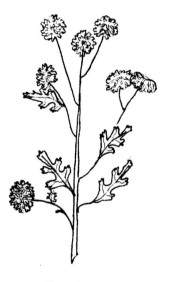

Feverfew

This plant has small white or gold double flowers with yellow centers, and blooms throughout the summer. Its wiry stems usually grow 1 to 1½ feet in height.

Cut the stems while the flowers are almost at their peak; then bundle them together and hang them upside down to dry.

Note: White Feverfew tends to dry a beige or ivory color, which makes it very popular in country floral decorations.

Flossflower
(*Ageratum*) (A)

Flossflower

This popular border flower is most commonly seen in shades of purple to blue-purple. However, varieties of pink, white, red, and gold are also available. The heights range from 6 inches to 2 feet, depending upon the variety. *Ageratum* continually blooms throughout the summer and fall.

Cut the stems when the flowers are in full bloom, strip off the leaves, bundle, and hang upside down or lay out flat to dry.

Gayfeather, Blazing Star
(*Liatris*) (P)

This plant has tightly compacted spikes in purple-rose, red-rose, or white, and grows from 1½ to 3 feet tall.

The spikes begin to fill out at the top of the stem (which is not the case with many spiky plants), and can be cut for drying when about three-fourths of the buds are open. At this point remove the leaves and hang the spikes upside down to dry.

Note: Air-dry only the colored varieties of this plant because the white variety will turn brown.

Gayfeather

Globe Amaranth
(*Gomphrena globosa*) (A)

Globe Amaranth

Gomphrena is a very popular flower for dried floral arrangements and wreaths. The plant has continuous cloverlike blooms of orange, purple, pink, or white. Two of the more common varieties are Cissy, a white bloom, and Buddy, a purple bloom. The plant height reaches about a foot.

Cut the stem just before the bloom reaches maturity, bundle, and hang upside down to dry.

Note: If there are several flowers left on the plant right before a frost when the season is nearly over, pull up the entire plant by its roots; then trim off the roots and hang the plant upside down to dry. Individual flowers or stems can then be removed at your leisure.

Globe Thistle
(*Echinops ritro*) (P)

This plant has globe-shaped flowers on sturdy 3- to 4-foot stems, and blooms during midsummer.

Cut the stems when the flower heads are just beginning to open; this is when they have their brightest blue coloring. Strip off the prickly leaves, bundle the stems together, and then hang them upside down to dry. (Although the stem on this plant may seem sturdy enough to stand upright in an open container for drying, the weight of the flower head would probably bow the stem.)

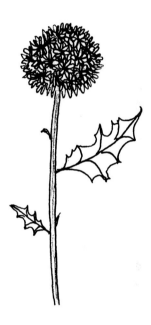

Globe Thistle

Goldenrod
(*Solidago*) (P)

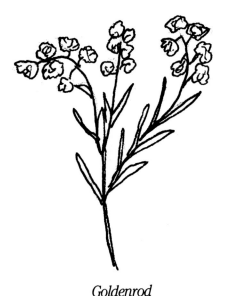

Goldenrod

The proper time for cutting Goldenrod is very important. You should cut this plant while the blooms are at their peak since the flowers do not open after they've been cut. However, make sure to cut before the blooms begin to brown. Cut the stems at a desired length, remove the leaves, band eight to twelve stems together, and then hang them upside down to dry.

According to folklore, this plant was used as a divining rod to find hidden treasures! Also, the plant was once thought to cause hay fever, but actually ragweed, which is in bloom at the same time, is the evildoer.

A bright golden wild flower, goldenrod grows to different heights depending upon the variety, and blooms from August through September.

Grapevines (V & P)

Grapevines are frequently used for making wreaths and adding an interesting touch to arrangements. (For tips on making Grapevine wreaths and other Grapevine decorations, turn to page 113.)

The best time to cut the vines is usually right after the first frost, when most of the leaves have fallen off. Try to cut the vines in long sections. If you don't use the vines soon after cutting, they will dry out and break as you try to intertwine them. If this happens, soak them in water to make them more pliable.

Grapevine

37

Grasses and Grains (A & P)

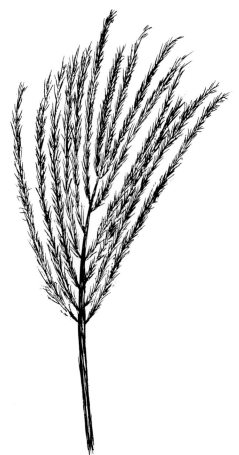

Zebra Grass

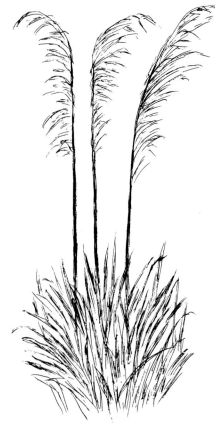

Plume Grass

There are many kinds of grasses and grains that can be used for decoration. Although we have devoted special sections to Pampas Grass (page 58) and Wheat (page 83), don't overlook other varieties of grasses and grains found growing along the roadside, along fence lines, and in fields. Some other good varieties of grass are Quaking Grass, Ribbon Grass, Squirreltail Grass, Pepper Grass, Fountain Grass, Zebra Grass, and Plume Grass (which is similar to Pampas Grass). Other grains to consider are Rye, Barley, and Oats.

Cut the grasses and grains so that you don't disturb the roots. Grasses and grains can be dried in two ways, depending on the look you want. If you hang them upside down, they will have stiff straight stems. If you want a curved, more casual look, place them in a tall vase or open container.

The right time to cut grasses and

Fountain Grass

grains is very important. If you cut them before they mature, they will dry a pale green as opposed to a pale beige.

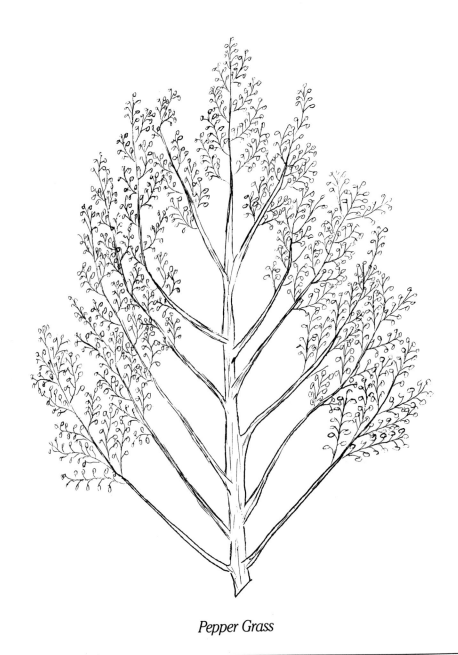

Pepper Grass

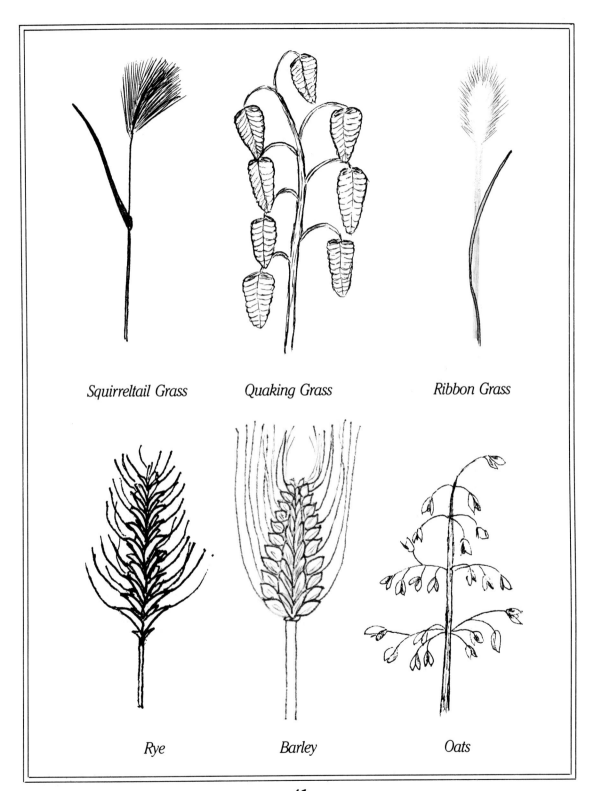

Squirreltail Grass   Quaking Grass   Ribbon Grass

Rye   Barley   Oats

Heath and Heather (S)

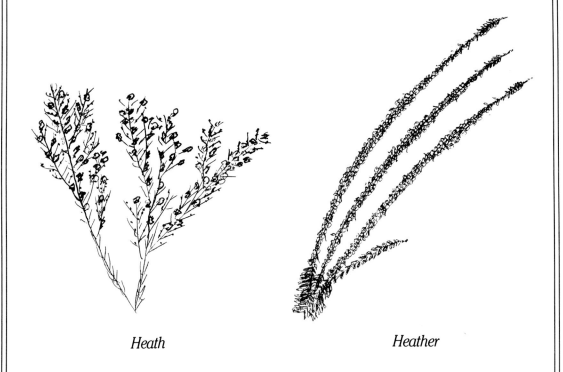

Heath

Heather

Heather and Heath closely resemble each other, although Heather is hardier. Both plants come in many varieties and several colors, and generally range in height from 1 to 2 feet. The flowers are densely compacted on wiry stems. Although Heather and Heath are grown more prevalently in warmer cli-mates, certain varieties of Heather have been adapted to colder environments.

You should cut the stems when the flowers are almost near their peak; then bundle the stems together and hang them upside down to dry.

Herbs (A & P)

Balm

Basil

Although we provide specific descriptions for certain herbs—such as Sage (*Salvia*) (page 68), Chives (*Allium*) (page 12), Eucalyptus (page 68), and Lavender (page 52)—don't be afraid to experiment with other herbs. You might consider using Basil, Balm, Camomile, Sweet Marjoram, Mint, Oregano, Pennyroyal, Rosemary, and Thyme. It's fun to grow these herbs, and they make an interesting addition to potpourri, wreaths, and floral arrangements. You can also hang herbs in bunches around your home, the way it was done centuries ago. The aromas emitted from many of these plants are wonderful!

Use the traditional drying method: Cut the stems, bundle them together, and then hang them upside down to dry. Herbs can also be wired while fresh onto straw wreaths or wire forms. After they have dried, you can add other decorations.

Camomile

Marjoram

Mint

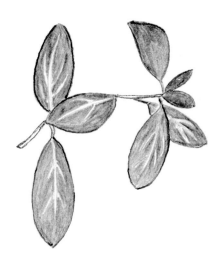

Oregano

Pennyroyal

Rosemary

Thyme

Hydrangea (S)

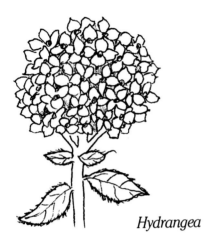

Hydrangea

Hydrangea grows from 4 feet to 9 feet tall, depending upon the variety. You can get hydrangea with flowers in all kinds of beautiful colors, such as crimson, blue, purples, pinks, and white. Always choose flower heads that are mature but still have their color.

The flowers can be dried in several different ways. You can lay them on a flat surface or hang them upside down. Or you can put them in a vase with a small amount of water that will gradually evaporate. Then the heads can be divided into smaller clusters to be used in arrangements.

Immortelle
(*Xeranthemum*) (A)

An everlasting herb of the daisy family, this plant grows 2 to 3 feet in height. The flowers are about 1½ inches in diameter, and bloom from July until the first frost. Colors include white, pink, lavender, and purple.

Cut the plant when the flowers are fully open; then bundle the stems together and hang them upside down to dry.

Immortelle

Joe-Pye Weed
(*Eupatorium maculatum*) (P)

Joe-Pye Weed

Joe-Pye Weed is a common wild flower that's partial to damp areas. In late summer, it's crowned with pretty flat-topped clusters of pale-purple flowers and reaches heights of 6 feet. Folklore has it that an American Indian named Joe Pye used this plant to cure fevers and Colonists used it to treat typhus.

Cut the stems before the buds open. (Should you cut the flowers while they are at their peak, they will disintegrate after drying.) Then bundle the stems together and hang them upside down to dry.

Lady's Mantle
(*Alchemilla*) (P)

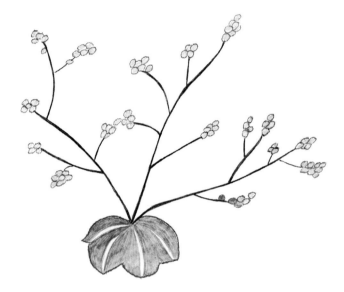

Lady's Mantle

This plant has evergreen foliage and small yellowish green flower-like blooms. It reaches a height of approximately 1½ feet.

Cut the mature stems; then bundle them together and hang them upside down to dry.

Note: Alchemilla is often grown as a ground cover because it spreads so rapidly.

Lamb's Ears
(*Stachys*) (P)

This plant has woolly, greenish grey leaves, from which stems of small purple flowers arise. It reaches heights of 1 to 3 feet, with the leaves becoming smaller as they climb the stem.

The best time to cut this plant for drying is before the tiny purple flowers bloom. Then you can bundle the stems together and hang them upside down to dry.

You can also cut individual leaves at varying times and lay them out flat to dry. The leaves are very delicate and tear easily when dry, so handle them with care when you use them in wreaths and arrangements.

One of the easiest and prettiest ways to use the leaves is to pin them all around a straw or moss-covered wreath immediately after cutting

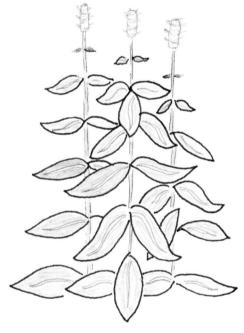

Lamb's Ears

them. (They should be evenly distributed and overlapping.) The leaves are easiest to work with right after cutting, and will dry on the wreath.

Larkspur, Annual Delphinium
(*Consolida orientalis,*
Delphinium ajacis) (A)

Larkspur

With its fragile appearance and delicate colors, dried Larkspur is a popular plant for floral arrangements. The plant ranges in height from 2 to 4 feet, and has blooms of pink, white, blue, or lavender.

When planting from seed, be sure to plant early enough because the seeds germinate best in cool weather. You can also plant the seeds in late autumn for blooms the following summer.

Larkspur should be cut for drying when all the flowers are open, except for those at the top 2 or 3 inches of the stem. Then hang the stems upside down or lay them out flat to dry.

Lavender
(*Lavandula angustifolia*) (P)

Lavender

Lavender is a fragrant herb that is commonly used in potpourri and sachets. It has grey-green leaves and small blue-purple flower spikes, and reaches heights of 1 to 4 feet.

You should cut lavender stems and leaves as soon as the flowers start to open; then hang them to dry in small bunches.

Love-in-a-Mist
(*Nigella damascena*) (A)

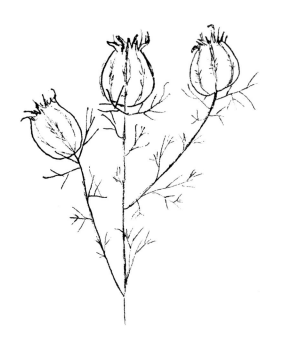

Love-in-a-Mist (pods and flower)

You can find *Nigella* flowers in shades of white, blue, purple, or pink on plants approximately 1½ feet tall. Persian Jewels is a good mixed variety. After the flowers bloom, the plant produces a decorative seed pod, which you can dry.

Cut the stems at desired lengths when the seed pods appear; then remove the leaves, bundle the stems together, and hang them upside down to dry.

Love-Lies-Bleeding, Tassel Flower (*Amaranthus caudatus*) (A)

Love-Lies-Bleeding

Amaranthus has prickly flowers in red and green, which droop from the tops of their stems during late summer through midfall. The plant grows to a height of 3 feet.

Cut the stems before the flowers are in full bloom; then strip off the leaves, band the stems together, and hang them upside down to dry.

Money Plant, Honesty
(*Lunaria*) (B)

Money Plant

Lunaria has fragrant white flowers that produce silver-white seed pods in late summer. The height of the plant ranges from 2 to 3 feet.

Cut the stems when the seed pods appear very dry, but have not begun to deteriorate. Then gently push back and forth on both sides of the pods with your thumb and forefinger. This will loosen the pods' outer surface, which you will then remove, thus exposing the silver-white membrane inside. (These pods also contain seeds, which you can dry and then plant the next growing season.) Stand the stems in an open container until you are ready to use them.

Orange Ball, Safflower
(*Carthamus tinctorius*) (A)

Orange Ball

This plant, often used as a source of red and yellow dyes, has fluffy, gold-orange, 1½-inch flowers, and reaches a height of 2 to 3 feet. It continually blooms throughout the growing season on stiff sturdy stems.

Cut the stems when the flowers are almost at their peak, bundle them together, and then hang them upside down to dry.

Ornamental Corn (A)

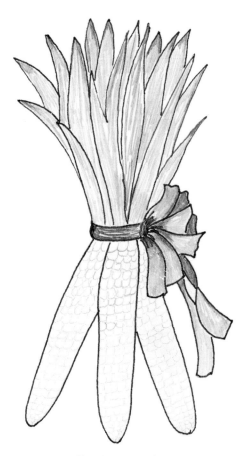

Ornamental Corn

Ornamental Corn comes in many colors and varieties.

When the ears are completely filled out, break them from the stalk. Do not pull the husks completely off, but pull them back away from the cob instead. Tie three ears together where the husks meet at the base of the ears and then immediately hang them for ornamentation.

Ornamental Corn is a popular autumn door decoration.

Ornamental Cotton (A)

Ornamental Cotton

Although Cotton is grown as a perennial in those parts of the American South where the climate permits, it is grown as an annual for ornamental purposes and out of necessity in the North.

Ornamental Cotton grows approximately 3 feet tall. It produces purple blooms in the spring and then fluffy white cotton bolls in the fall. In colder climates, you may need to start the seeds indoors in early spring since Cotton requires a long growing season.

Cut the fluffy white open bolls at maturity, when they produce seeds surrounded by Cotton fibre. Then place them in an open container until you're ready to use them.

Ornamental Cotton makes an unusual and interesting addition to arrangements and wreaths.

Pampas Grass (*Cortaderia selloana*) (P)

In late summer this grass produces large pink or white plumes on stems that grow approximately 4 feet tall.

Cut the stems in early fall, as soon as the plume has reached maturity. If you wait too long to cut, the plume will shed after you dry it. After cutting the stems, stand them upright in a large open container.

Pampas Grass

59

Pearly Everlasting
(*Anaphalis*) (P)

Pearly Everlasting

This plant has small white flowers with yellow centers, and stems approximately 12 inches tall. It blooms during the summer and early fall.

Cut the stem at the base when the yellow centers begin to show in the top flower clusters. Or, if you prefer an all-white effect, cut before the centers begin to turn yellow. Then band the stems together in small bunches and hang them upside down to dry.

Note: With this particular plant, it's easier to strip off the leaves after the plant has dried.

Peony
(*Paeonia*) (P & S)

Peony

Peonies are beautiful bushy plants that come in white, pinks, and reds. They grow up to 3 feet tall, and have profuse blooms from mid- to late spring.

Cut some of the stems when the flowers are just beginning to open, and others when the flowers are still buds. An arrangement tends to be more interesting if you use both slightly opened flowers and buds.

Hang the stems upside down to dry in small bunches. You will need to dry Peonies for a minimum of 3 to 4 weeks because of their densely compacted petals. When dried, Peonies resemble large Roses and have a wonderful long-lasting scent. White Peonies dry a creamy yellow, a color that particularly enhances floral country decorating.

Peppers, Hot Reds (A)

Peppers

Red-pepper varieties—such as Cayenne, Jalapeño, and Anaheim—produce peppers that grow from 1 to 8 inches long.

To dry the peppers, string the stems on string or wire. These pepper strands can be an attractive ornamentation in a kitchen, and you can break off the dried peppers and use them in cooking.

To create a pepper wreath, directly pin the peppers onto a straw wreath or wire them onto a wreath form, and then let them dry.

Pods

Whether gathered from your garden or from out in the wild, many types of plant pods look beautiful in dried floral creations. If you would like the pods to have a shinier or more enriched appearance, you may want to try varnishing or shellacking them. However, you should experiment with various pods because some don't react well to this treatment.

Although there are many pod-

Pods

producing plants, here is a partial list of some of the most common ones.

- Bellflower
- Black-Eyed Susan
- Bouncing Bet, or Soapwort
- Butterfly Weed
- Cinquefoil
- Coneflower
- Cotton
- Cucumber, wild
- Evening Primrose
- Field Pennycress
- Foxglove Beard-Tongue
- Ground-Cherry
- Heal-All
- Horsemint
- Iris, wild
- Love-in-a-Mist
- Milkweed
- Mullein
- Poppy
- Queen Anne's Lace
- Rattlesnake Master
- Thimbleweed
- Toadflax

Pussy Willow
(*Salix discolor*) (S)

Pussy Willow

This shrub can reach heights of 12 feet or more. In early spring, the branches produce fuzzy nibs called catkins.

Cut the branches as soon as these silver-white catkins develop. This keeps the height of the Pussy Willow in check, and also promotes a healthier shrub. After cutting the branches, you can immediately enjoy them in a vase or an open container.

From left: decorated basket, decorated box, and door swag

Heart-shaped Willow wreath, traditional wreath, and door swag

Grapevine wreath with berries, decorated baskets, and country hat

Clockwise from top: decorated basket, small topiary tree, country hat, twig bundle, and nosegay

Queen Anne's Lace, Wild Carrot (*Daucus carota*) (P)

This wild flower has large, lacy, white flower heads, and can grow up to 5 feet tall.

Cut the stems when the white flowers are in full bloom. Because of the head size, hang this plant in small bundles for drying. Another drying method involves using a piece of chicken wire. Attach the wire on both sides, and allow for enough room underneath so that the stems can be placed through the holes in the wire. The large heads will then lie flat on top of the wire until they are dry.

Queen Anne's Lace

Note: If you have waited until it's too late to cut the flowers, the skel- etons that remain can be cut and used in dried floral creations.

Rhodanthe
(*Helipterum manglesii*) (A)

Rhodanthe

This plant produces lovely rosy pink flowers surrounded by silver petals and grows about 18 inches high.

Cut the stems before the flowers are fully open; then bundle them together and hang them upside down to dry. You can also place a piece of florist wire into the base of the partially closed bud (follow the instructions for Strawflowers on pages 74–75).

Roses (P)

All varieties and colors of Roses can be used for drying, depending on your personal preference.

First, cut the head while it is still in the bud stage, just before it's ready to open. Then loop a wire through the green base on the bottom of the Rose, and hang it upside down to dry for at least 4 weeks. Another method involves leaving about ⅛ inch of the stem on the bud and pushing a piece of florist wire up into it; the stem will then dry tightly on the wire. However, you should still hang the Rose upside down by the wire for drying so that the Rose will retain its shape.

Note: Keep in mind that all Roses

Rose

turn at least a shade darker when dried; so, dark-red Roses will turn black.

Salvia (*X superba*) (P);
Blue Sage, Blue Salvia (A)

Salvia

Salvia has flower spikes of white, blue, or purple, and grows 2 to 3 feet tall.

Cut at the base of the stem when all but one inch of the flowers at the top of the spike are open. Then bundle the spikes together and hang them upside down to dry.

Silver Dollar Plant (*Eucalyptus*) (T)

Eucalyptus has very aromatic, silvery green leaves, and tends to thrive in warmer climates. In colder climates, you can grow this tree in a pot outdoors in the summer and then indoors the rest of the year—or indoors year-round. Two varieties we recommend for drying are *Eucalyptus cinerea* (more commonly seen in florist shops) and

Eucalyptus globulus. Cinerea has round leaves, while *globulus* has more elongated leaves.

Cut the stems and then hang them upside down or lay them out flat to dry. When air-drying the *cinerea* variety, you'll see that the branches with the smaller leaves dry best. For the larger leaves, you may need to use glycerin for preservation. *Eucalyptus* is very popular the year-round, but even more so at Christmastime. Because of its scent and color, it can be a lovely addition to Pine boughs.

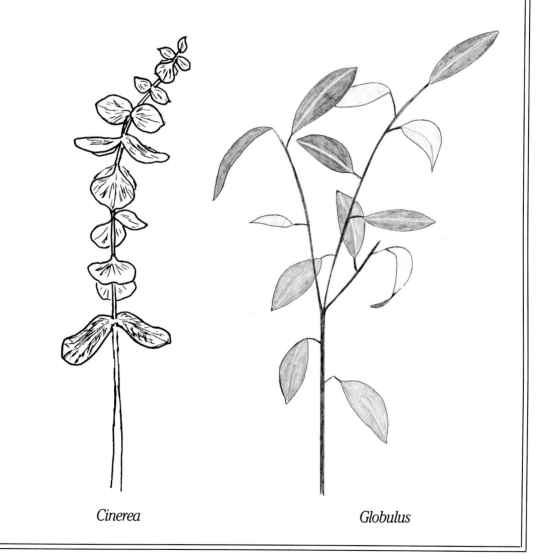

Cinerea   Globulus

69

Starflower
(*Scabiosa stellata*) (A)

Starflower

Starflowers have light-brown flower heads, comprised of tiny florets with dark star-shaped centers. These flower heads grow about 1½ inches in diameter.

Cut when the heads are fully developed with tiny florets. Then band the stems together and hang them upside down to dry.

Statice, Sea Lavender
(*Limonium*) (A & P)

Of the everlastings, Statice is one of the most colorful and easiest to grow. The plant's popularity dates back to the early gardens of colonial Virginia.

Limonium sinuatum (A) This plant has a versatile papery flower, which dries exceptionally well, keeping its bright clear color. The flower colors include white, yellow, buff, apricot, pink, rose, lavender, purple, and dark bluish purple. Two popular varieties are Art Shades, with its many pastel colors, and Pa-

Limonium sinuatum

Limonium suworowii

Limonium bonduelli

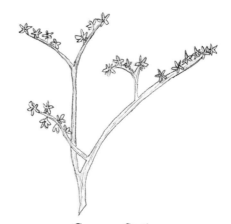

German Statice

cific Giants, a colorful mixture in deeper, more vibrant shades. Heights range from 9 to 24 inches.

***Limonium suworowii* (A)** This plant has rose-pink flower spikes that grow to a height of 9 inches.

***Limonium bonduelli* (A or B)** This plant has yellow flowers that grow in branched clusters with oval leaves.

German Statice (*Limonium tataricum*) (P) This plant has

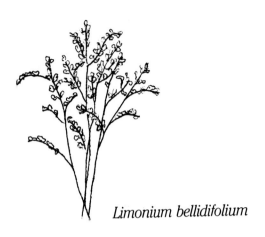

Limonium bellidifolium

Limonium bellidifolium (P)
This final variety has sprays of delicate mauve flowers growing on stiff stems.

You should cut all varieties when the flowers are at their peak. (Overripe blossoms will shed when dried.) Band 6 to 12 stems together; then hang them upside down to dry.

Note: You can also stand German Statice in an open container for drying. The flowers will have a fuller appearance when dried in this manner.

white tiny flowers that grow on stiff stems to heights of 9 to 18 inches, and blooms during July and August. It's used extensively by florists.

Stock
(*Matthiola*) (B)

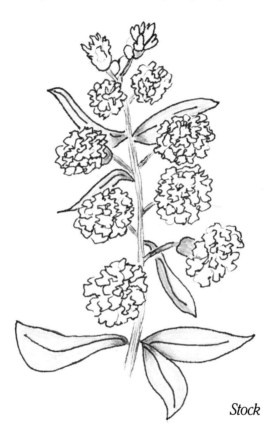

Stock

Stock's flower formation is similar to that of Larkspur. Stock is fast to germinate, has long-lasting compacted blooms, and reaches heights of 1 to 2½ feet. It can be found in a beautiful array of colors, which include red, blue, purple, pink, rose, and white. The double variety is best for air drying.

Cut Stock while most of the flowers are in bloom, but not yet at their peak. (The flowers will shrink dramatically.) Then bundle the stems together and hang them upside down to dry.

Strawflowers
(*Helichrysum*) (A)

One way to dry Strawflowers involves removing the leaves from the bottom of the bud and then pushing a piece of florist wire into it.

Strawflowers

This plant is available in a wide range of colors. Heights range from 1 foot for the dwarf variety (Bikinis) to 4 feet. Because of the everlasting beauty of its flowers, *Helichrysum* was often used in funeral wreaths.

It's best to cut off the bud when it is less than one-fourth open or even still closed since the bud will open during drying. When you harvest Strawflowers, just snip off the bud. The plant will then continue to bloom right up until the first frost.

Strawflowers on florist wire

74

Be careful not to push it in too far, as the wire will then show when the bud opens during drying. Stand the wires upright during the drying process; sticking the wires into a large piece of plastic foam or a container of sand works well. Another way of drying Strawflowers is to push the florist wire sideways through the base of the buds, stringing several on one piece of wire. If you want a stemmed multi-floral effect, start with a large bud and work upwards, ending with a tiny bud. Or you can string several of the same-size buds together, bend the wire in a circle, and con- nect both ends to form a mini- wreath; then you can add a bow or ribbon. You can also cut the stems at desired lengths, bundle them to- gether, and then hang them upside down to dry. However, you will not get as many flowers from the plant with this method.

Note: When using the wire method, place the bud on the wire as soon after picking as possible. If you wait too long, the base of the bud will dry out and will be difficult to place on the wire. Since the bud will always dry tightly on the wire, make certain you have the flower in the desired position before drying.

Strawflower mini-wreath

Sunray
(*Acroclinium, Helipterum*) (A)

Sunray

This variety of *Helipterum* has beautiful small daisylike blooms, which can be found in pale pink, bright pink, salmon, and white, with bright-yellow centers. It grows as high as 24 inches.

When the buds are closed, but you can determine the color of the flower on about a half of the bud, cut the stems and hang them upside down to dry. The bud will open while drying.

However, because these stems are delicate, it's best to dry them by placing a piece of florist wire into the base of the bud. First remove the leaves from the bottom of the bud and then push the florist wire into it. Be careful not to push it too far, as the wire will then show when the bud opens during drying. Stand the wires upright during the drying process. Sticking the wires into a large piece of plastic foam or a container of sand works well.

76

Tansy, Bitter Button
(*Tanacetum*) (P)

Tansy

Tansy has flower heads that are small, yellow, and buttonlike, and grow in flat-topped clusters on sturdy 2- to 3-foot stems.

The plant grows well in dry unattended areas, such as between railroad ties. The leaves have a strong sharp aroma, and were once used to flavor teas.

Cut the stems before the buttonlike flowers become too full. If cut too late, the flowers will develop a brown tinge but can still be used. Remove the foliage, band the stems together, and then hang them upside down to dry.

Teasel
(*Dipsacus*) (B)

Teasel

Teasel is a coarse thistlelike herb. You can grow it in your garden or find it along the roadside from early summer until autumn. It can reach heights of up to 5 feet. The flowers are pale lilac.

Cut the stems near the base of the plant, bundle the stems together, and then hang them upside down to dry until needed.

Florists sometimes dye teasel bright colors for arrangements.

Note: You may wish to wear gloves when gathering Teasel because of its prickly formation.

Thrift
(*Armeria*) (P)

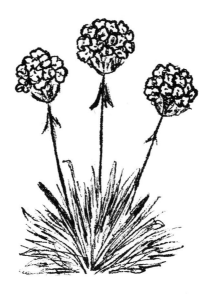

Thrift

Armeria is a type of ground cover with green grasslike foliage. It has numerous small round flower heads, which come in white, pink, and rose. Some good varieties to use for drying are Ornament, a mix of the three colors mentioned, and Snowball, which is white. This plant blooms several times throughout the spring and summer.

Cut the thin stems, bundle them together, and then hang them upside down to dry.

Note: Armeria has rather fragile flowers. Should the heads fall off the stems, you can glue them to wreaths or use them in potpourri.

Tickweed, Sunray
(*Coreopsis*) (P)

Tickweed

Coreopsis grows to heights of 2 to 3 feet, and has golden-yellow flowers as large as 2½ inches in diameter. These wild flowers bloom throughout the summer and fall.

Cut the flowers when they are in full bloom and then hang them upside down to dry. The flowers will shrink dramatically to pretty, bright golden buttons.

Note: Keep in mind that during and after drying, these flowers are very susceptible to humidity. If you don't use or keep them in a dry area, you should forgo harvesting them for use in dried wreaths or arrangements.

Toadflax
(*Linaria*) (A)

Toadflax

This plant has pungent small flowers on long narrow stems, and grows about 6 to 9 inches tall. The flowers resemble miniature Snapdragons in shades of purple, red, orange, gold, and white. They have a very long blooming period, usually beginning in June and continuing into August. *Linaria* does well in dry areas, and it's easy to replant the next growing season if you save some of the dry seeds.

Cut this plant while it's in full bloom; then band the stems together and hang them upside down to dry.

Vines (P)

Many types of vines can be used in dried-flower decor. In addition to Grapevines or Bittersweet vines, you might consider Clematis, Trumpet Honeysuckle, Wisteria, and Climbing Hydrangea.

Cut the vines at their longest possible lengths; then put them in a pile or hang them on hooks or nails until you are ready to use them. Soak the vines in water if they have become too dry and brittle to work with.

Bittersweet vine

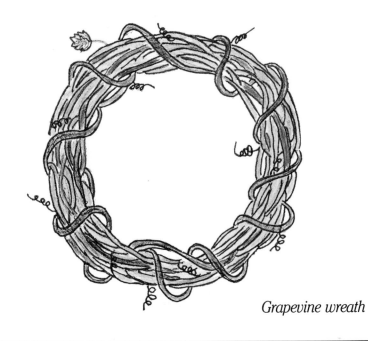

Grapevine wreath

Wheat
(*Triticum*) (A or B)

Wheat

Wheat is often dyed or sprayed, but you may prefer the original straw color for more natural decorating. At Christmastime it's a Scandinavian custom to tie together wheat bundles, or *Jule Negs*, and then hang them outside on a fence post or a tree for the birds.

Wheat is a cereal grain, which matures in mid-June.

Timing is an important factor when cutting wheat. You should cut it when the beard is golden but the base of the stem is still green. This way, the wheat will be much more durable and will last much longer. Cut the stems near the base and stand them up in a tall open container until you need them.

Wheat bundle

Willow (T)

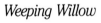

Weeping Willow

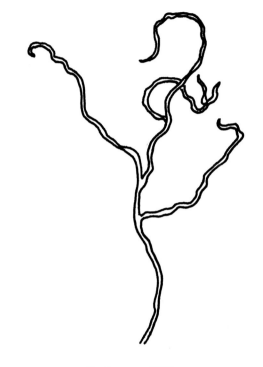

Corkscrew Willow

The Weeping Willow tree has drooping, graceful branches that trail to the ground. It's most frequently found along rivers and around lakes.

Because the Willow's branches are so thin and pliable, you can easily form them into all kinds of interesting shapes and then dry them. For example, you can cut several branches, strip off the leaves, and then tie them into a bow. After placing a flat weight, such as a board or a cardboard box filled with sand or rocks, on top of them, allow the branches to dry for a minimum of 3 weeks. This dried-Willow bow makes a lovely country accent on a wall. Or you can create a wreath by cutting several branches at their longest possible lengths. Then strip off the leaves and follow the instructions for creating a Grapevine wreath on page 113. Willow branches can also be banded together with wire to form a heart. Leave the ends long so that the heart wreath has long graceful tails. Place a weight on top of the heart. Also, the gnarled branches from a Corkscrew Willow make a fascinating addition to dried floral arrangements.

Remember to let any of your Willow creations dry for a minimum of 3 weeks.

Willow bow

Winged Everlasting
(*Ammobium*) (A)

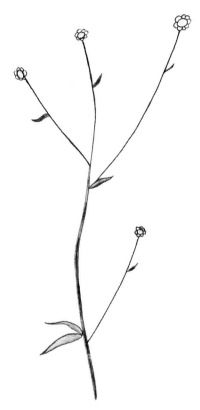

Winged Everlasting

A large variety of *Ammobium*, Grandiflorum tends to work best for air drying. This plant has small white flowers with yellow centers, grows to a height of 3 feet, and blooms from midsummer to late fall.

Cut the white flowers before the yellow centers appear; otherwise, the centers will be dark after drying. Then band the stems together and hang them upside down to dry.

Wormwood
(*Artemisia*) (P)

Silver King—first stage

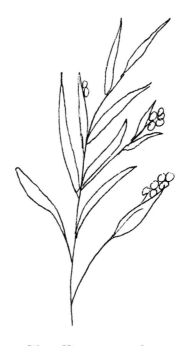

Silver King—second stage

Silver King   With its silvery grey aromatic foliage, Silver King is the best variety of *Artemisia* to use for drying. The plant reaches heights of 2 to 3 feet.

Silver King can be cut at two stages of growth. It can be cut during early summer when the leaves are more compacted and larger, but it's more commonly cut later when the tiny flowers are in bloom and the leaves are smaller and more graduated in size. You can cut at both stages for two different effects.

Then band the stems together and hang them upside down to dry.

Note: Since Silver King is a rapid spreader, you should plant it in an area where its root runners will not interfere with other plants.

Dusty Miller This variety of *Artemisia* is commonly grown as an annual where we live in the American Midwest. Because of its silver foliage, it's frequently used as a border plant.

You can cut the stems throughout the summer. After cutting, band the stems together and hang them upside down to dry.

Dusty Miller

Note: According to ancient folklore, if you hang a bundle of *Artemisia* above your door it will dispel evil.

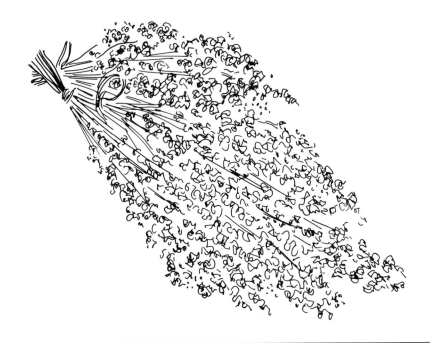

Yarrow
(*Achillea*) (P)

The following are a few of the more commonly found varieties of *Achillea*.

Ballerina This plant has pure-white double flowers on sturdy stems that range from 6 to 8 inches. Ballerina is especially attractive as a border plant because of its profuse sprays of flowers, which bloom throughout the summer.

The Pearl This plant has small double white flower clusters, which bloom from spring until fall. It grows approximately 2 feet tall.

Moonshine This plant has large golden clustered heads on thick sturdy stems, and grows up to 4 feet tall. The flowers bloom in July and August.

With the Moonshine variety, you should cut the plant when the golden heads are fully open, but before they start to turn brown (although some people also find the brown heads desirable).

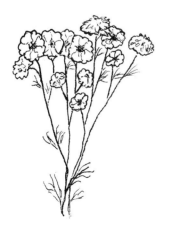

Ballerina

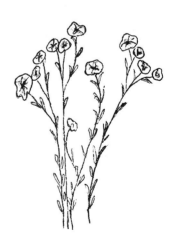

The Pearl

Moonshine

Achillea millefolium

Achillea millefolium   A wild variety of Yarrow, this plant has large white flat-topped heads and grows about 3 feet tall. It's an especially good plant to use for drying.

Fire King   This variety has large deep-red flat heads, and grows to heights of 2½ to 3 feet.

For all of these kinds of *Achillea*, cut the stems at desired lengths when the flowers are in full bloom, strip off the leaves, bundle the stems together, and then hang them upside down to dry.

Fire King

Note: Achillea can be a vigorous spreader, so you may want to plant it in an area where it can take over.

3
WAYS TO USE
DRIED FLOWERS

We originally began growing our own flowers to cut down on the high cost of dried materials. But, as a result, we've also ended up with an abundant supply of flowers at our disposal. Now, after years of experimenting with different ways to use dried flowers, we would like to share some ideas with you.

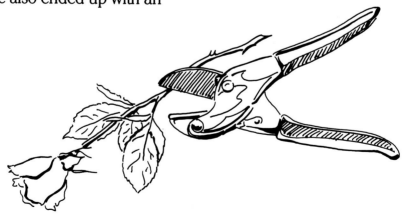

By the Stem

Dried flowers, by the stem

One of the easiest ways to display dried materials is to hang them in bundles (the way they were dried) on doors, walls, or open beams around the house. They can be secured with a ribbon or a bow, giving the house added warmth and charm as well as a traditional country-style feeling.

If you wish to make a profit from flower drying, you can sell your dried materials by the stem. Properly dried home-grown everlastings are often more desirable than everlastings sold in stores. They usually have more vibrant colors, and they don't tend to shed as easily. They are also not flattened out or damaged, as is often the case with store-bought flowers due to shipping. You can sell dried flowers at crafts fairs and country markets, and even to florists.

Potpourri

Another way to use all kinds of dried flowers is in a potpourri. Select some of your more aromatic plants and then, after drying them, crumble the flower heads and leaves together in a large bowl or container. It looks prettier if you leave some flower heads whole. Roses can be an especially appealing and fragrant addition. If you use Lavender, be careful because a little of its scent goes a long way.

To enhance the natural scents of your flowers, you may want to add a drop of your favorite fragrance oil or a pinch of your favorite herbs and spices. (Do not use powdered herbs or spices.) You may also want to use a fixative to help the fragrance last longer. A common fragrance fixative, or extender, is Orrisroot, although other fixatives are also available. Use approximately one tablespoon of Orrisroot per quart of dried materials.

You can use all kinds of combinations of flowers, herbs, and spices in a potpourri, but keep in mind their scent and texture as well as their color. You might want to conjure up a potpourri from the following lists of ingredients:

Flowers
Roses
Delphinium
Larkspur
Feverfew
Strawflowers

Herbs
Lavender
Rosemary
Mint
Thyme
Lemon Balm

Spices
Cloves
Cinnamon
Nutmeg
Allspice
Anise

Potpourri is as personal as perfume. After a little experimentation, you'll find a scent to suit your individual taste.

Wreaths

Dried floral wreath

The wreath is the most traditional form of decorating with dried materials. It is a favorite of ours, probably because the circle is symbolic of friendship and good luck. You can also make heart-shaped wreaths, which are, of course, symbolic of love. After a little bit of practice with design and technique, you'll be surprised at the beautiful wreaths you will be able to create.

You'll need these materials to make a dried floral wreath:

- straw wreath form,
- pole pins,

- Spanish Moss, and
- dried flowers and foliage.

You can find straw wreath forms, pole pins, and Spanish Moss at florist and crafts shops. If this is your first wreath, start out small with an 8- or 10-inch wreath form.

First decide what flowers and foliage you want to combine. Have an ample supply on hand so that you don't run out before the wreath is finished. The stems on the flowers don't have to be any longer than 1½ inches, but it's easier to snap the stems at the desired lengths while you are working.

Next, cover the front side of the straw wreath with a thin layer of Spanish Moss. This is not a necessity, but it will give the wreath a much more finished appearance when completed. Glue on the Moss or use a few pole pins to hold it in place. You don't need to be too par-ticular in the way you tack the Moss to the form because the Moss will become secured tightly when you pin on the flowers.

Combine a small bunch of flowers and foliage. Using a pole pin, attach the small bunch by its stems to the straw wreath. Start at the middle of the left side of the form, working across and counter-clockwise.

Fan the small bunches of flowers while pinning the stems to the form. Overlap the flowers on top of the stems as you work downwards covering the stems and pole pins. Alternate as many different kinds of flowers and foliage as desired, but try to keep a fairly uniform pattern. Continue working all around the wreath in this manner. If there are any open spots upon completion, push or glue a few more flowers into these spaces. For a final touch, add a bow or ribbon streamers.

Floral Arrangements

Dried floral arrangement

Entire books are devoted to floral arranging, but in this section we will give you very basic instructions so that you can begin creating some lovely dried-flower arrangements. First of all, a general rule in floral arranging is that the arrangement should be one and one-half times taller than its container. It's also helpful to keep in mind that the most common shape in floral arranging is the triangle.

When you are using a fairly tall, narrow container, you can arrange dried flowers the same way you would arrange fresh flowers. But remember that it will take more dried flowers to create an arrangement because dried flowers have less density than fresh flowers.

When creating an arrangement in a shallower, more open container, such as a basket or a bowl, you will need the following supplies:

- container,
- plastic foam,
- florist wire (22-gauge),
- glue or two-sided floral tape,
- green florist tape,
- Moss (green or Spanish), and
- dried flowers and foliage.

After selecting a container, cut a piece of foam so that it's the same width and height as your container. You may need to use two or three thicknesses, depending upon the container's height, or you can cheat by placing newspaper under the foam in the bottom of the container. Secure the foam to the bottom or sides with either glue or two-sided

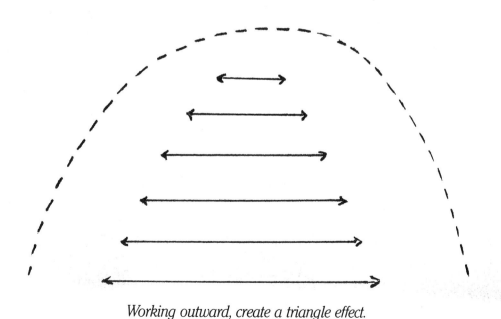

Working outward, create a triangle effect.

97

floral tape. The tape is not a permanent adhesive the way glue is, so you can easily remove the arrange-

Wrap the tape around the natural stem and the florist wire.

ment at a later date should you want to use the container for something else.

Next, spread a very thin layer of Moss over the foam, and then anchor it by gluing the edges.

Select flowers with sturdy stems; otherwise, the stems will break when you stick them into the foam.

Flowers with weak stems will need to be restemmed. Do this by cutting off the flower head, but keeping about ¼ to ½ inch of the natural stem left on. Cut the florist wire to the desired length, and then place it up under the base of the flower head and against the small natural stem. Unroll a strip of the florist tape, but do not cut it off the roll yet. Stretch the section of the tape. Then begin wrapping the tape, from the base of the flower head, around the natural stem and the florist wire. Continue wrapping down the wire, twisting with your thumb and index finger as you go. When you have reached the end of the wire, tear off the tape. The reason for taping the wire is to make it stick more securely in the foam. Unwrapped wires tend to loosen.

After you have fixed the weak stems, decide which flowers will be the most dominant in the arrangement. Start by sticking four of them into the foam in the center of the container. Fill in around these four flowers with other flowers and filler (possibly Baby's Breath). Then cut the next stems shorter as you are working towards the outside of the container to create a triangle effect.

When you have completed the arrangement, hang some flowers or foliage over the edge of the container to create a more natural look. Then you can add a bow or ribbon streamers. To dust or freshen the arrangement, spritz it occasionally with a fine mist of water.

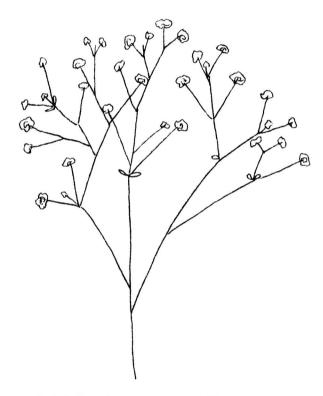

Baby's Breath makes a good filler.

Decorated Baskets

Decorated basket

Easy-to-make decorated baskets are another way to use everlastings, especially the smaller flowers and buds. The basket can be any shape, small or large, with or without a handle.

First, glue a thin layer of Spanish Moss along the rim of the basket. When the Moss dries, glue on a filler type of flower, such as Baby's Breath or German Statice. The next step is to fill in the rim with small flowers. Some of our favorites to use are Strawflowers, Rosebuds, and Globe Amaranth (*Gomphrena*). You can create a colorful mixture or choose flowers of a predominant color to match a decor.

The basket can be finished with a bow.

You can give a basket a seasonal look, depending on your choice of flowers. For the Christmas season, use a little greenery and red flowers. Spring and Easter call for pastels. You can use a larger basket for Easter eggs. Summertime usually means brighter and more colorful flowers, and autumn lends itself to golds, oranges, and browns.

These baskets look pretty anywhere in a home. You can use them to hold potpourri, soaps, make-up, or letters—or leave them empty and use them for decoration.

Decorated Boxes

Decorated box

You can easily decorate wood or cardboard boxes with dried flowers. The boxes can be found at crafts and variety shops in varying sizes and shapes (round, oval, heart). They are sometimes nested, one inside the other, three to a set. Any number of items can be stored in these boxes—jewels, sewing accessories, soaps, and potpourri, to name just a few. The boxes look very attractive placed on a dressing, vanity, or sofa table. If you put small doilies inside a box, you will have created a coaster set. Also, these decorated boxes make excellent gifts.

The outside of the box can be left plain, or you may want to paint it or stencil it. The box can even be covered with wrapping paper, wallpaper, or ribbon.

Before covering the lid with small dried flowers and buds, you may want to attach a small handle in the center. To make the handle, wrap a piece of wire with ribbon and then form it into the shape of a ring. Keep in mind that a portion of the ring will be hidden in the flowers, so make sure the ring is large enough to be easily manipulated.

Now begin gluing on your flowers, covering the entire lid. If preferred, you can glue on a thin layer of moss prior to gluing on the flowers. Your flowers can match or complement your room decor or they can be seasonal.

Country Hats

To add a country touch to any home decor, place a hat decorated with assorted dried materials on a door, wall, clothes tree, or bedpost. Smaller hats can be incorporated into wall groupings, and miniature ones can be used as Christmas ornaments. (Of course, you can also create a country hat to be worn as an accessory with a spring or summer outfit.)

Since hats come in so many styles and sizes, these instructions will be somewhat general.

To create a country hat, you will need the following supplies:

- hat,
- ribbon,
- glue,
- thin wire, and
- assorted dried materials.

Cut a piece of ribbon to fit around the crown of the hat, and glue it in place. You can then apply Spanish Moss, but this is optional. After deciding which flowers you are going to use, distribute five of the largest ones evenly on the hat around the ribbon. Make sure to leave a space for the bow. Fill in around the five larger flowers with the remaining flowers. Leaves or ferns can also look attractive. We suggest first arranging the flowers on the hat and then gluing them down after you have achieved the effect you want. Finally, glue on the ribbon streamers and the bow in the open space. If you are going to hang the hat, bend a piece of florist wire into a ring and then glue it to the inside brim.

Here are a few suggestions in terms of flowers. To create an elegant look, we recommend using Roses, ferns, and Baby's Breath. A more traditional country hat can be decorated with Yarrow, herbs, and Feverfew. For a colorful look, try using Statice and Strawflowers as the predominant flower combination.

Start with five of the largest flowers, leaving a space for the bow.

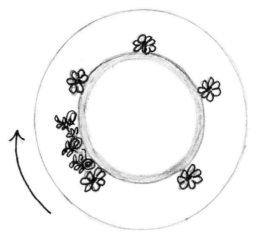

Add the remaining flowers.

Complete the hat with ribbon streamers and a bow.

Dried Floral Collages

Dried floral collages, or pictures, are a unique way to use your creative talents. Shaped like bouquets, wreaths, or hearts, these collages can be preserved for years under glass. They are a three-dimensional alternative to pressed-flower pictures; however, the colors of pressed flowers seem to fade rather quickly, whereas these vibrant colors tend to last a long time.

Dried floral collages make a special gift for any flower lover. They can be used as wall decorations, set on dressers, tables, shelves, and bathroom vanities, or placed upright in china cabinets.

Wreaths You will need the following supplies to create a wreath-shaped picture:

- colored or white sketching paper,
- shadow-box or glass-domed frame,
- glue, and
- small dried flowers.

Before you begin making the picture, break up the flowers into smaller pieces and cut off the stems. If you are using Baby's Breath or German Statice, you will only need the tip of the branch. Statice can be broken into small florets.

To start, place a circular object, such as a glass, in the middle of the paper and, using it as a template, lightly draw around it with a pencil.

Then cover the pencilled circle with flowers. German Statice and Baby's Breath work well on colored paper, but create little contrast against white paper. On white paper, Larkspur is a good alternative. When you glue the flowers on, overlap them slightly in both directions to give the wreath a wispy look. After these flowers have dried, glue the other flowers on top of them, taking care to watch color and spacing. Then you can add a small bow with streamers of coordinating colors.

Hearts To make heart-shaped pictures, basically follow the instructions for the wreaths. Of course, omit the part about drawing a circle, and draw an outline of a heart instead. You can leave the middle open, creating a heart-shaped wreath, or fill in the entire shape with flowers. If you leave the middle open, you might want to write a short message or just the word "Love."

Bouquets To make a bouquet collage, you will need:

- colored or white sketching paper,
- shadow-box or glass-domed frame,
- glue,
- ferns, and
- flowers.

For this type of picture, leave some of the flowers whole with stems. Start by gluing five to eight ferns (depending on the size of the frame) in an oval pattern in the middle of the paper. Inside of and partially covering the ferns, fill in the oval with flowers. Make sure some of the stems come down beneath the arrangement to create the appearance of a bouquet. Then add a ribbon around the stems as a finishing touch.

To make a wreath-shaped picture, first draw a circle and then cover it with flowers.

With a circular or heart-shaped wreath collage, you can write a short message in the middle.

To make a bouquet collage, start with ferns.

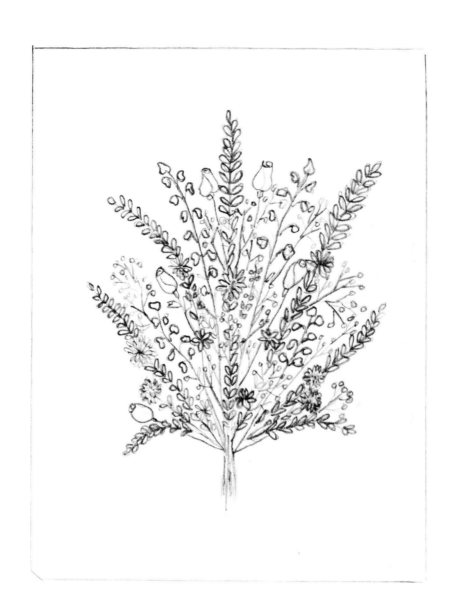

Then fill in the shape with flowers.

Centerpieces and Other Table Decorations

Dried floral topiary tree

Instead of decorating your table with the usual flower arrangements, try some of these unique dried floral creations. Incidentally, if you create some of the centerpieces for a special event, you can raffle them off or give them out as door prizes.

Hurricane Candle Rings Beautiful candle rings can be created using dried materials. However, we suggest you contain the candles and candleholders in hurricane glass because of the danger of fire. Even when using hurricane glass, we are hesitant about lighting the candles. Let common sense be your guide.

Cut a plastic-foam ring so that it will fit around the hurricane glass. Before inserting the flowers, you may want to cover the plastic foam with moss. Use any kind of dried flowers or foliage. If the flowers have delicate stems, restem them. You may want to restem the flowers on toothpicks rather than florist wire.

You can further decorate these candle rings to accent a particular decor, season, holiday, or event—such as a wedding, anniversary, or shower.

Dried Floral Topiary Resembling topiary trees, these small dried floral trees add a fanciful accent to a table. As with the candle rings just described, you can further decorate these little trees any way you desire.

To make dried floral topiary, you will need the following supplies:

- plastic-foam ball,
- plastic foam,
- stick or wood dowel,
- round basket or container without a handle,
- glue,
- ribbon, and
- dried materials.

Begin by cutting a piece of plastic foam to the size of your container. Tack it to the inside of the container with two-sided floral tape or glue. Insert a wood dowel or stick into the center of the plastic foam. If you use a dowel instead of a stick, you can wrap the dowel with ribbon. Cover the top of the plastic foam in the container with dried green foliage or moss. Next, glue moss around the plastic-foam ball, and insert it on the stick or dowel. Then begin gluing flowers all around the ball. When you have completed your tree, add ribbon and a bow around the container itself or directly around the stick or dowel.

You can make these dried floral trees any size you desire. If you make large ones, put a weight in the bottom of the container to prevent the tree from becoming top-heavy and tipping over.

Twig or Cinnamon-Stick Bundles Cut some twigs at least a foot long and bundle them together, or bundle together some long cinnamon sticks. Bind them tightly together in the center with a thin piece of wire. Cover the wire by gluing on a band of ribbon. Glue moss or dried foliage in the center of the bundle; add filler such as Baby's Breath or German Statice, and then some dried flowers. Use any of the smaller flowers, such as Strawflowers, Roses, Helipterum,

Limonium sinuata, Feverfew, and Globe Amaranth. Leave at least 3 inches of the twigs or cinnamon sticks showing on each end, with your floral arrangement in the middle. For an additional decorative touch, you can attach a small artificial bird and a bird's nest directly to the twigs or sticks in the center of the arrangement. Or you can attach Pinecones to give the arrangement a Christmas flair. Complete the dried floral bundle with a bow.

Floral Cornucopia Instead of filling the traditional cornucopia with fruit, make a lovely fall arrangement using dried grasses, grains, and flowers in autumn colors.

Place-Setting Baskets At your next dinner party, fill little individual baskets with dried materials for each place setting. You can put place cards in these baskets. Or you can glue small dried flowers and pretty little ribbons around the outside of the baskets, and fill each basket with mints. Give each of your guests a little basket as a gift.

Grapevine Creations

Wreaths Grapevines can be crafted into many unique shapes (we've seen them formed into rabbits, geese, hearts, and sleighs), but they are most commonly used in wreaths. A Grapevine wreath adds rustic charm to country decorating.

After you have cut the vines into the longest lengths possible, determine the circumference of your wreath. Then bend one length of the vine into a circle. Lap it a couple of times, and then pull the long end through the circle and start overlapping and intertwining it. Keep doing this until you've used up all of the vine. Then tuck in the end of the vine and continue with a new vine, wrapping and overlapping until you've created a wreath in the thickness you desire. It may take several lengths of vine to make one wreath.

A Grapevine wreath provides a natural background for dried flowers. You can weave them

Keep wrapping and intertwining until you form a wreath.

113

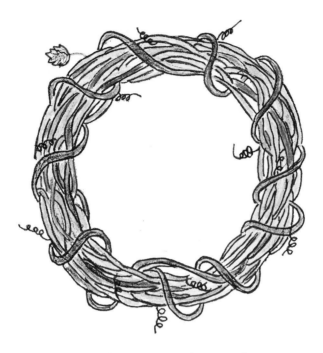

Completed Grapevine wreath

through the Grapevines or attach them on the wreath with glue or wire. Use as many flowers as you like, depending on the effect you want. For a more rustic and finished look, first glue Spanish Moss on the wreath and then glue or wire the flowers over it. You can complete the wreath with a bow. A bow made of Raffia can add an attractive touch. You can buy Raffia by the braid in crafts and florist shops.

Christmas Trees Another attractive creation you can make with Grapevines is a Christmas tree, which is always a charming addition to holiday-season decorating.

First, you will have to construct a form for the tree in the shape of a cone. For this, you'll need four slats of wood and two bottom cross pieces. Use two pieces of 12"-long, ¾"-thick, and 1"-wide wood for the base. Form and nail them into a cross shape (X). For the uprights, use four slats that are ¾" thick, 1" wide, and 2′ long. Nail a slat to each end of the cross, and then draw and wire the slats together at the top to form a cone.

After you have constructed the form, secure one end of the vine at the form's base with wire. Begin circling the form with the vines at the base, wrapping and overlapping while working upwards. Do not leave gaps so that you can see through the tree. When you run out of vine, tuck the end in and then start with a new vine. Continue doing this until you have covered the entire form. The natural irregularities in Grapevines give them their special appeal, so don't cut off any of the little spiral shoots.

Now you can decorate the tree with dried flowers, ribbons, or traditional Christmas-tree ornaments.

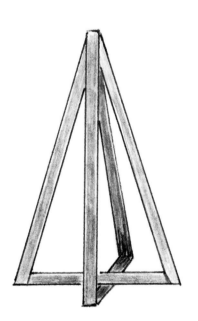

Form for Grapevine Christmas tree

Grapevine Christmas tree

A Country Christmas

Here are some additional ideas to brighten the Christmas season.

Decorating the Christmas Tree
Enhance your Christmas tree with beautiful dried flowers! First stick bunches of flowers between the boughs of the tree and then add your ornaments. A Christmas tree decorated with Baby's Breath, German Statice, and white Hydrangea is always very attractive. For a Victorian look, use Baby's Breath in pale blues and mauves, and lots of lace and satin ribbon. Or you might want to use a combination of bright colorful flowers. The flowers should enrich or enhance your tree and ornaments; they should not, however, be overpowering.

Decorated Christmas tree

Christmas garland

Christmas Garland You can create a Christmas garland using Boxwood, fresh Pine boughs, or other available greenery by wiring the branches together. (If this greenery is not available, you can buy artificial garland.) Then wire dried materials, such as Eucalyptus, Baby's Breath, Roses, and German Statice into the greenery. Plastic Holly berries, Pinecones, nuts, Acorns, and ribbons can also be wired or glued in for more variety.

Garlands draped around doors, windows, railings, or cupboards create an old-fashioned Christmas atmosphere.

Everlasting Christmas Ornaments Dried-flower ornaments are unique and fun to make.

Here's a list of the supplies you will need:

• green plastic foam (2½ to 3 inches in diameter),
• glue,
• ribbon,
• wax paper,
• straight pins, and
• dried flowers.

Begin by removing the stems from the dried flowers. Then pour some glue onto a piece of wax paper. (Do not use a hot glue gun, unless you put glue on the flower first rather than applying hot glue directly to the plastic foam.) Dip each flower into the glue and then press it onto the plastic-foam ball. Continue in this manner until the ball is covered with flowers. Now take a piece of thin ribbon and make a small bow with tails, and pin it into the top of the ball. Cut another piece of ribbon to be used as a hanger. Loop this ribbon over and pin it on top of the bow. You might want to add a drop of glue to the tip of the pin for added security.

These ornaments can be made with potpourri instead of flowers. Roll the ball in glue and then in your potpourri, making sure that it's evenly distributed. Add your ribbon and hanger in the same manner as described for the flower ornaments. You now have a beautifully scented ornament to hang on your tree or give as a gift.

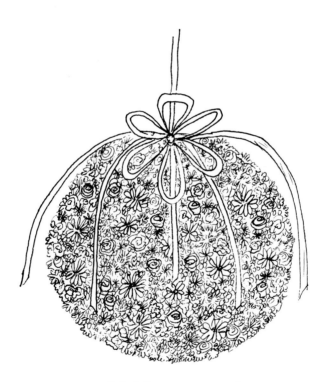

Dried-flower ornament

Nosegays

Nosegay

Did you know that flowers have a unique symbolism? Folklore indicates that people have been communicating by the use of flowers since medieval times. A small bouquet of flowers called a nosegay (or tussie-mussie) is still used to express a range of qualities and meanings. It generally contains particularly aromatic flowers and herbs, which reveal a message when given to a loved one.

These plants are said to convey the following meanings.

Artemisia   *safekeeping*

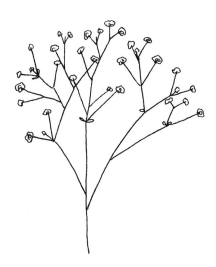

Baby's Breath   *fertility, gaiety*

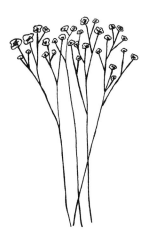

Celosia   *faith, unfading love and devotion*

Broom Bloom   *humility, neatness*

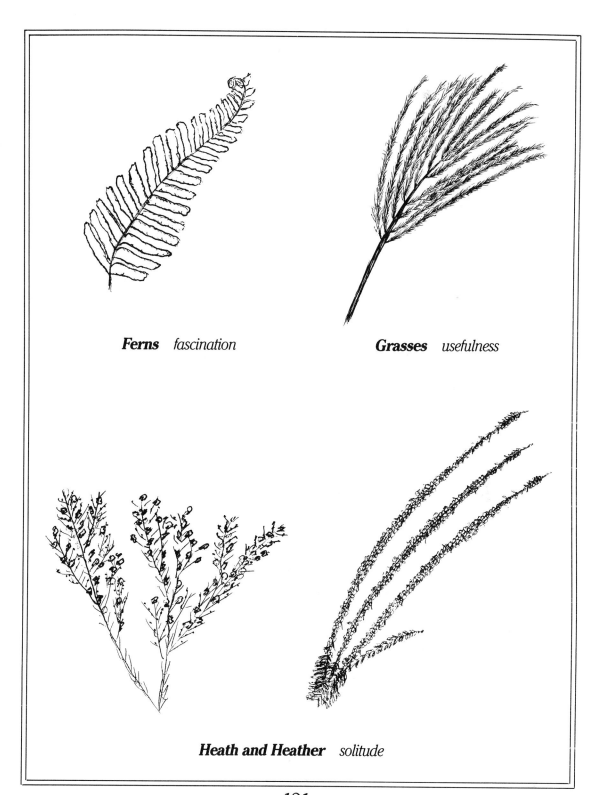

Ferns *fascination*

Grasses *usefulness*

Heath and Heather *solitude*

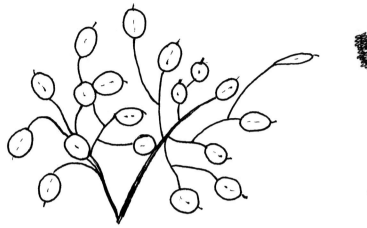

Honesty, Lunaria *forgetfulness*

Lavender *distrust*

Love-Lies-Bleeding *hopelessness, desertion*

Rosebud *youthful beauty*

Rosemary *grace, remembrance*

Statice *everlasting remembrance*

Wheat *sacrifice*

There are several different styles of nosegays, but we will describe just a few of our favorites. Although you can make them with any dried materials, your nosegay will be extra special if it conveys a particular message or meaning.

One style consists of a very small bouquet encircled by a lace doily or a band of lace. First cut the stems so that they are only 2 to 4 inches long; then wrap them with florist tape or wire. Cut a slit or small round hole in a lace doily and insert the wrapped stems, or encircle the bouquet in a band of lace. Glue the stems to the doily or band of lace to hold them in place. For a finishing touch, tie ribbon streamers around the wrapped stems.

Using this same method, but on a smaller scale, you can make country or Victorian Christmas-tree ornaments. Make the bouquets no more than 3 inches in diameter, with the stems no more than an inch long. Glue a strip of ribbon to the wrapped stems, and connect both ends of the ribbon to form a loop. This loop will enable you to hang the nosegay on a Christmas tree. Cut a slit or hole in a tiny lace doily and insert the wrapped stems, or encircle the small bouquet in a strip of lace. Then tack the lace to the wrapped stems with glue. You may also have to do a little sewing to help tack down some of the gathering around the stems.

The final style requires some work, but the end result will be well worth your effort.

Here is a list of supplies you will need (bear in mind that the dimensions are approximate, and depend on the size of the nosegay you want to create):

- 6-inch piece of florist wire, 20-gauge or heavier;
- small block of wood approximately 1½″ × ¼″;
- ¼-inch-thick piece of plastic foam, cut to the size of the wood block;
- 6-inch lace doily;
- ribbon;
- glue; and
- dried materials.

First drill a tiny hole in the middle of the block of wood. Then glue the plastic foam to the opposite side of the wood. Starting in the middle with stems approximately 3 inches long, insert the flowers in the plastic foam. If the stems are flimsy, they will need to be restemmed (refer to page 98). Create a triangle effect by using the longer stems in the middle and gradually shortening the stems as you work towards the outside. You may want to use a little glue to help hold the stems in place since the plastic foam is so thin.

Glue the block of wood containing your bouquet in the middle of the doily. Also, glue the doily to the edges of the block. This will hold the doily upright around the bouquet of flowers. Wrap the 6-inch length of florist wire with ribbon. Poking through the doily, find the hole that was drilled into the bottom of the wood block, and then insert and glue the ribbon-wrapped florist wire. Bend the end of the wire on the bottom to resemble an umbrella handle. Add ribbon streamers and your nosegay will be complete.

By making a nosegay with this small piece of wood inserted in the middle, it can lie on an angle with less weight on the side of the bouquet. Thus, the flowers will not become flattened or crushed on that side, and will lie nicely on a vanity, dresser, or table.

More "Flower Power"

Door swag

- Combine Wheat and/or other grains with Strawflowers and grasses. Tie them together with an "autumn"-colored bow. Then hang them upside down as a swag.
- Fill little muslin bags or netting with potpourri, and tie them together with ribbon.
- Imagine a country wedding decorated with everlastings: the bouquets, hats, headpieces, and flower girls' baskets. There would be no wilting, and the wedding memories would be "everlasting."
- Add color to your houseplants by sticking in a few colorful sprays of dried flowers.

- Instead of using a bow on a gift-wrapped package, glue on a little dried-flower bouquet or arrangement.
- Spread greenery and dried flowers across a piece of plastic in the middle of a table for a party or buffet. At Christmastime, add Pinecones and artificial red berries.
- Also, during the Christmas holidays, decorate a Pine or Balsam wreath (fresh or artificial) with bows, dried flowers, and Pinecones.

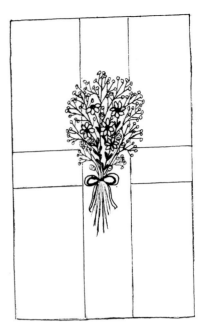

Gift-wrapped box

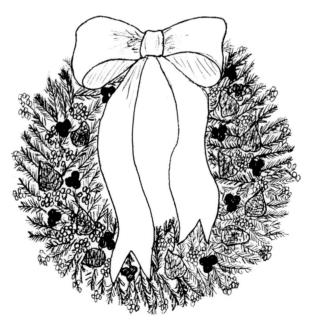

Decorated Pine wreath

Index

Achillea, 89–90
Ageratum, 32
Alchemilla, 49
Allium, 12–13
Amaranthus caudatus, 54, 122
Ammobium, 86
Anaphalis, 60
Annual, 11
Annual Delphinium, 51
Armeria, 79
Arrangements, floral, 96–99
Artemisia, 87–88, 120
Asparagus, 13
Astilbe, 29
Baby's Breath, 6, 7, 14, 120
Bachelor Button, 25
Ballerina, 89
Balm, 43–44
Barley, 41
Basil, 43–44
Baskets, decorated, 100
Bells of Ireland, 15
Biennial, 11
Bitter Button, 77
Bittersweet, 16
Bittersweet Vine, 82
Blazing Star, 32–33
Blue Sage, 68
Blue Salvia, 68
Bouquet collage, 105, 108–109
Boxes, 101, 126
Boxwood, 17
Broom, 18, 120

Broomcorn, 19
Buxus, 17
Camomile, 44
Candle rings, hurricane, 111
Carthamus tinctorius, 56
Cattails, 20–21
Cayenne Pepper, 62
Celastrus, 16
Celosia, 22–23, 120
Centaurea, 25
Centerpieces, 110–112
Chinese Lantern, 24
Chive, 12
Christmas-tree decorations,
    116–118
Christmas trees, Grapevine,
    114–115
Chrysanthemum parthenium, 31
Cinerea, 69
Cinnamon-stick bundles, 112
Cockscomb, 22–23
Collages, dried floral, 104–105
Consolida orientalis, 51
Corkscrew Willow, 84
Corn, Ornamental, 57
Cornflower, 25
Cortaderia selloana, 58–59
Country Christmas ideas, 116–118
Country hats, 102–103
Crested Cockscomb, 22
Cutting of plants, 11
Cystisus scoparius, 18
Daucus carota, 63, 65

Delphinium, 26
Delphinium ajacis, 51
Dipsacus, 78
Dock, 27
Door swag, 125
Drumstick Allium, 12
Drying space, limited, 8–9
Dusty Miller, 88
Echinops ritro, 35
Edelweiss, 28
Eucalyptus, 68–69
Eupatorium maculatum, 48
False Goat's-Beard, 29
Ferns, 30, 121
Feverfew, 31
Fire King, 90
Floral arrangements, 96–99
Flossflower, 32
Fountain Grass, 39
Garland, Christmas, 117
Gayfeather, 32–33
German Statice, 71–72
Globe Amaranth, 6, 7, 34
Globe Thistle, 35
Globulus, 69
Glycerin, 9
Goldenrod, 36
Gomphrena globosa, 34
Grains, 38–41
    Wheat, 83, 123
Grapevine(s), 37
    creations using, 113–115
Grasses, 38–41, 121

Gypsophila, 6, 7, 14, 120
Hats, country, 102–103
Heart-shaped floral collages, 105, 107
Heath, 42, 121
Heather, 42, 121
Helichrysum, 74
Helipterum, 47
Helipterum manglesii, 66
Herbs, 43–45
Honesty, 55, 122
Hot Reds, 62
Hurricane candle rings, 111
Hydrangea, 46
Immortelle, 47
Jalapeno, 62
Joe-Pye Weed, 48
Korean Boxwood, 17
Lady's Mantle, 49
Lamb's Ears, 50
Larkspur, 51
Lavender, 52, 122
Leatherleaf Fern, 30
Leontopodium alpinum, 28
Liatris, 32–33
Limonium, 70–72
Love-in-a-Mist, 53, 63
Love-Lies-Bleeding, 54, 122
Lunaria, 55, 63, 122
Macrocephala, 25
Maidenhair Fern, 30
Marjoram, 44
Matricaria, 31
Matthiola, 73
Meadowsweet, 29
Mint, 44
Moluccella laevis, 15
Money Plant, 55, 122
Moonshine, 89–90
Nigella damascena, 53

Nosegays, 119–125
Oats, 41
Orange Ball, 56
Oregano, 44
Ornamental Corn, 57
Ornamental Cotton, 58
Paeonia, 61
Pampas Grass, 58–59
Pearl, 89
Pearly Everlasting, 60
Pennyroyal, 45
Peony, 61
Pepper Grass, 40
Peppers, 62
Perennial, 11
Physalis franchetii, 24
Plumed Cockscomb, 22
Plume Grass, 38–39
Pods, 63
Potpourri, 93
Pussy Willow, 64
Quaking Grass, 41
Queen Anne's Lace, 63, 65
Red Peppers, 62
Reeds, 20–21
Rhodanthe, 66
Ribbon Grass, 41
Rosebud, 122
Rosemary, 45, 123
Roses, 67
Rubber bands, 9
Rumex, 27
Rye, 41
Safflower, 56
Salix discolor, 64
Salvia, 68
Scabiosa stellata, 70
Scotch Broom, 18
Sea Lavender, 70–72
Silver Dollar Plant, 68–69

Silver King, 87–88
Solidago, 36
Sorghum vulgare technicum, 19
Sprengeri Fern, 30
Squirreltail Grass, 41
Stachys, 50
Starflower, 70
Statice, 6, 7, 70–72, 123
Stem, displaying flowers by, 92
Stock, 73
Strawflowers, 6, 7, 74–75
Sunray, 76
Supplies, 9
Table decorations, 110–112
Tansy, 77
Tassel Flower, 54, 122
Teasel, 78
Thrift, 79
Thyme, 45
Tickweed, 80
Toadflax, 81
Topiary tree, 110–112
Triticum, 83
Twig bundles, 112
Typha latifolia, 20–21
Vines, 82
Weeping Willow, 84
Wheat, 83, 123
Wild Carrot, 63, 65
Willow, 84–85
Winged Everlasting, 86
Wormwood, 87–88
Wreaths, 75, 94–95, 113–114, 126
Wreath-shaped collage, 104, 106
Xeranthemum, 47
X superba, 68
Yarrow, 89–90
Yellow Broom, 18
Zebra grass, 38–39